Poet Kathleen Housley deftly navigates the confluence of science, art and theology, helping the reader see each of those defining streams of our humanity as emerging from the single source of the Creator. But in so doing, she is just as often pointing out how each jostles and intrudes on the others as she is describing their flow towards unification in a new creation.
    Mark Sprinkle, *Bio Logos*

Kathleen Housley's elegantly crafted poems satisfy and delight on multiple levels. With Epiphanies we are led to unexpected places where the scientific, the creative and the sacred intertwine, thus giving rise to questions but as well revealing surprising connections and joyous possibilities for contemporary men and women. Drawing from anthropology, mythology, paleontology, biology and history, among others, these poems speak in many voices, not the least of which is that of Leonardo da Vinci, in character as both artist and scientist. Kathleen Housley, with grace and no small portion of wry humor, has created intelligent, complex work that is often touching, frequently exciting, and always accessible. No small feat! Ultimately, Epiphanies is a jubilant collection.
    Alexandrina Sergio, author of *My Daughter Is Drummer in the Rock'n Roll Band* and *That's How The Light Gets In*.

EPIPHANIES

OTHER BOOKS BY THE WISING UP PRESS COLLECTIVE

Keys to the Kingdom: Reflections on Music and the Mind
Kathleen L. Housley

Live Your Life & Other Stories
Only Beautiful & Other Stories
Kerry Langan

Last Flight Out: Living, Loving & Leaving
Phyllis A. Langton

A Hymn that Meanders
Maria Nazos

Germs of Truth
The Sanctity of the Moment: Poems from Four Decades
Visible Signs
Heather Tosteson

ALSO BY KATHLEEN L. HOUSLEY

The Letter Kills But the Spirit Gives Life, the Smiths
Emily Hall Tremaine: Collector on the Cusp
Tranquil Power: The Art and Life of Perle Fine
Black Sand: The History of Titanium
Firmament

EPIPHANIES

KATHLEEN L. HOUSLEY

Wising Up Press Collective
Wising Up Press
Decatur, Georgia

Wising Up Press
P.O. Box 2122
Decatur, GA 30031-2122
www.universaltable.org

Copyright © 2013 by Kathleen L. Housley

All rights reserved. No part of this book may be used or reproduced in any manner whatsoever without written permission, except in the case of brief quotations embodied in critical articles or reviews.

Catalogue-in-Publication data is on file with the Library of Congress.
LCCN: 2013948205

Wising Up ISBN: 978-0-9827262-9-7

TABLE OF CONTENTS

I. AND WE ARE NOT SAVED

Addendum to the Peace Treaty	2
Demotion	3
Psalm for a New Human Species	5
The Softest Yarn	7
Pavane for a Dead Rover	9
Cold Comfort	10
Millipede	11
St. Ex	12
Driving the Ambulance With Robert Frost	13
Cardiac Arrest	15
Dementia's Museum	16
The Mathematician's Wife Ponders Ontology	18
Psych Ward	22
The Landing Place	23

II. PRAYER BOOK FOR AN INFLUENZA PANDEMIC

Avian Flu, A Prayer of Petition	26
H1N1, A Prayer of Adoration	28
Spanish Flu, A Prayer of Forgiveness	29
Swine Flu, A Prayer of Confession	30
Ferret Flu, A Prayer of Thanksgiving	31
A Prayer of Commemoration	32
A Benediction	34

III. THE ART OF SCIENCE, THE SCIENCE OF ART: LEONARDO DA VINCI

The Painting of Wings	36
The Drawing of Dragons	41
The Painting of Water	47
The Painting of Infinity	52

NOTES	59
ACKNOWLEDGEMENTS	62

AND WE ARE NOT SAVED

ADDENDUM TO THE PEACE TREATY

When you beat your swords into ploughshares,
leave the maker's symbol on the reshaped blades.
Let tripwires twine like tendrils around new rakes,
and triggers jut awkwardly from the handles of spades.
As an incongruous reminder that pruning hooks
can be beaten back into spears, use a munitions case
for a planter exploding with red poppies. Water well.

DEMOTION

Get wisdom, get understanding.
Proverbs 4:5

In ninth grade biology class back in the dawn of time,
my teacher taught us that we were all classified
as *Homo sapiens sapiens,* meaning doubly wise,
smarter than smart, the best of all creatures
who walked the face of the earth, having dominion
over lesser life-forms that didn't have a single *sapiens,*
let alone two, as part of their genus-species names,
evolution and natural selection having conspired
with Almighty Providence to place us fifteen-year-olds
(even Kenny "the Missing Link" Shapiro) just above
the great apes on the tree of life, though my mediocre grades
made clear there was room for improvement even at the top.

Blessed to be young in the Holocene's balmy days,
blissfully unaware of glacial melt and rising seas,
I went on to earn a living and procreate my superior kind,
and aside from browsing through waiting-room copies
of *National Geographic* for updates on Olduvai Gorge,
I fell behind the times, which explains my surprise
on hearing the news that I am living in a new epoch,
the Anthropocene. What's more, my species name
is in question because gene sequencing has revealed
a percentage of my nuclear DNA can be traced back
to Neanderthals, those heavy-browed cave folk
who carried clubs and are supposed to be extinct.

Having given up dominion, settling for just getting by,
I am now in danger of demotion, reduced to *Homo*
without a *sapiens* to my baleful name, lumped into
the tribe *Hominin,* a term that sounds very like *homonym*
signifying a word with many meanings and various truths,
such as the word *fluke* that is at one and the same time
a parasitic flatworm, a bottom-dwelling flounder,
a whale's tail fin, a part of an anchor, a chance event.
Out of context, meaning is severed from its mooring
and wisdom is set adrift among the flatworm-flounder-fins
of anchored chance leaving behind one regrettable truth:
I never was able to live up to my name.

PSALM FOR A NEW HUMAN SPECIES

What was *Homo floresiensis*
that you were mindful of her,
walking upright in the shadow
of a volcano on the third island
east of Bali, a mere 18,000 years ago,
if electron spin resonance and
radiocarbon luminescence be true?
Was your name majestic
in the rainforest's green depth
when you gave her kind dominion
over your peculiar menagerie:
pygmy elephants, komodo dragons,
giant tortoises, and strange fauna
drifting eastward on the sea's paths
to create new Edens where wombats
gestated their young in pouches,
and honeyeaters whistled staccato?

If, as it is written, you made man
but a little lower than the angels,
putting all things beneath his feet,
what do you want me, *Homo sapiens*,
to do with her—my little sister,
barely a meter tall, whose soft bones
were found in a limestone cave
covered by volcanic ash? I thought
my brawling-sprawling forebears
were the last *Homo* species standing.
But now, like a lovechild from your
wilder youth, she appears, offering

proof of kinship based on brain size,
the morphology of her wrist bones,
compelling me to wonder: what
immutable transgression locked
her kind into paradise, and mine out.

THE SOFTEST YARN

All Trina wants is a new pair of socks
just like her old ones made from the softest yarn
by a cousin in Finland who knows how
to knit and purl a cable stitch
that ensnares a glint of the midnight sun
a pastel wave of the Northern lights,
far lovelier than is necessary for
the prosaic task of warming toes
on nights of deepening cold;
for though unnoted by mapmakers,
the Arctic Circle has shifted south
under the glacial weight of Trina's stroke,
shattering her words into shards of ice
and locking her muscles in permafrost.

So we begin our search for the softest yarn
to send to her cousin in time for Christmas,
on a drizzly day threatening snow;
more like an expedition than a shopping trip,
that requires hefting the wheelchair into the trunk,
angling Trina's rigid leg around the doorframe,
adjusting the seat belt over the sling,
tucking a pillow under her clenched fist,
while I silently question the wisdom of it all.
Already she is exhausted, and we have not left,
but her yearning wells up from an inner aquifer
that never runs dry, having the power
to propel us even if I never turn the key—
a yearning not truly for socks
but for the ability to put them on alone.

Braving the hazards of wet roads,
curbs, steps, and uneven pavement,
we finally make our way into the store
only to find the aisles so overflowing with yarn,
the wheelchair cannot pass, so Trina resorts
to her cane and my arm, stepping sideways
with her left foot and dragging her right,
step-thunk, step-thunk, gleeful and giddy
among the lush colors of merino wool,
alpaca, and mohair, coming from the Andes,
the pastures of Iceland, the valleys of Wales,
and nearer to home, the hills of Vermont,
bulky yarn for a heavy fisherman's sweater,
baby-weight yarn for a newborn's blanket,
long skeins looped over the backs of chairs,
balls in baskets, displays of buttons,
and needles rising up like leafless stems in jars
waiting to knit their own blossoms.

Trina murmurs *oh, oh, oh* over and over,
touching the wool lightly with her fingertips.
When a clerk asks her what she is seeking,
she answers by pulling from her pocket one sock,
saying simply "*this,*" and is handed a golden skein
flecked with the blues and pinks of dawn and dusk.
She says *yes* with passionate finality, too tired to go on,
knowing it is time to bind off, willing into that *yes*
the strength to keep socks and self from unraveling,
the light from dimming, snow from falling. Too late,
we travel home through slush, bringing with us,
while there is yet time, the softest yarn.

PAVANE FOR A DEAD ROVER

Nothing human about you, little *Spirit*,
only six but full of self. For three years
you have been silent, embedded in soft dirt
on Mars while we wait here on Earth,
hoping that with the return of spring,
the strengthening light will fall directly
on your solar panels, cleaned at last
of reflective dust by strong winds,
resurrecting your dead batteries,
so that once again you flood our screens
with data on mineral-rich rocks dredged
from a volcanic plateau named Homeplate,
the last place you were seen alive —
if we can use that word for you.

You are our titanium Scott, our lithium Byrd,
who when your computer chips were down,
braved your own elements and persevered,
dragging your locked wheel in a slow dance,
like a pavane through an empty kingdom.
How can we not anthropomorphize you?
The contrary one who didn't follow commands,
draining yourself with too much work
even when you were told to sleep.
Yet until the end, you sent us dispatches
from a newer world, like Tennyson's Ulysses,
made weak by time and fate, but strong in will,
to strive, to seek, to find, and not to yield.

COLD COMFORT

The way Herod liked to listen to John the Baptist,
summoning him from his cell for private chats
but could make no sense of what he said;

the way Festus kept Paul locked up for two years
because he enjoyed hearing him talk,
although his words made him afraid;

the way the German guards, terrified by night bombings,
sought out Pastor Bonhoeffer even though he was,
by his own account, a provider of cold comfort—

writing to a friend, "I can listen all right,
but hardly ever find anything to say.
Yet perhaps the way one asks about some things
and is silent about others helps to suggest
what really matters"—

none of those ways could stop
the sharp rap on the prison door
or the words "come with us"

        as if for one more quiet conversation
        about what really matters.

MILLIPEDE

Holy Spirit: do not descend as a dove.
Better to return as a millipede hidden
beneath decaying bark than anything
that can soar. Ponder the incarnational
worth of *Pneumodesmus newmani*,
the oldest known form of life on land,
linking *air breathing* with the surname
of the Scottish bus driver and amateur
paleontologist who chiseled its fossil
from harbor rocks north of Stonehaven,
observing through his field lens small
openings in its exoskeleton used
for inspiration, meaning it moved its
many legs on dry ground, not seabed.
Or consider this descendent of *Pneumo*,
younger by four hundred million years,
curled for self-preservation on my palm,
a hard button of red legs whorled inward,
circled by dark armor plate, both of us
breathing air while we wait for a sign
that it is safe to resume whatever it was
we were scurrying to do prior to this
disruption of our forward flow to make
a theological point: Of what use are
metaphors of flight for things with feet?

ST. EX

They have found you at last, my little prince,
on the bottom of the sea with bullets in your wings,
for evidence, a silver bracelet engraved
with your name snagged in a fisherman's net.

Corsair of cyclones high in the Andes,
paladin of mail routes through desert storms,
you took to heart your friend's prophetic words,
"It's worth it, it's worth the final smash-up."

Men concerned with matters of consequence
could not keep you from flying reconnaissance
one more time near Marseille; battered and stiff,
an easy mark despite your evasive loops.

Since then, I have memorized "the loneliest
saddest landscape in the world." I have watched
under the star where you vanished, longing
to learn if the sheep has eaten your rose.

DRIVING THE AMBULANCE WITH ROBERT FROST

Emergency room, 3:30 a.m.,
hustle of stretcher, abrupt light,
hiss of air pressure apparatus,
as doctors and nurses converge
and hover around a woman with
emphysema frantic for breath;

then back into the silence of night
and a nor'easter gathering strength
just off the New England coast,
assaulting the rig with heavy flakes
and transforming familiar roads into
narrow corridors never traveled;

while the driver, face dimly lit by
dashboard glow, begins to recite
whose woods these are I think I know
to the EMT slumped with fatigue
in the passenger seat, and pauses at
promises to keep, the words sustaining,

lovely, dark and deep, like breath at last
flowing easily through scarred lungs,
or the brief reassurance of a reflector
confirming the road's unseen way,
as the soft shush shush of the wipers
rhythmically tempts to sleep,

and is resolutely refused, for miles
and miles, through silent forests,
vanishing towns—no tracks in the storm
but the rig's own, filling up with snow.

CARDIAC ARREST

She will be buried with the print of my hand
bruised into her chest, placed there before she slid
beyond my assault on her failing heart
that refused to resume its ninety-year beat
even when shocked; her lungs equally averse,
as if they were implacable witnesses to their own end.

Sleet rattled the windows as I knelt on the floor,
wishing I could spare her defibrillation's onslaught
so she could go in peace without lights and sirens,
wearing her fuzzy slippers and pink flannel nightgown,
her gaze fixed on a wall calendar serenely empty of days.

DEMENTIA'S MUSEUM

Open after hours,
no fee.

    Dawdle by a rickety
        display case
        lit by flickering
        light bulbs
        shards of childhood
        pinned on faded velvet.

    Tour a musty alcove
        titled "lovers"
        rusty nails
        clean squares of wall
        where pictures
        once hung.

    Hear faint laughter
        pilfered by the wind
        children playing
        on a distant swing
        rising, falling,
        falling.

    Touch a chipped plate
        edged in blue
        beside a tarnished

    silver spoon
    monogrammed
    without letters.

Who has hidden
the key?

THE MATHEMATICIAN'S WIFE PONDERS ONTOLOGY

The fundamental philosophical concept is cause.
It involves will, force, enjoyment, God, time, space.
The affirmation of being is the cause of the world.
                              Kurt Gödel

I have no head for numbers, counting on my fingers
when adding up the grocery bills. Yet it calmed Kurt
when I encouraged him to talk about his theorems,
the two of us sitting at the kitchen table, the sunlight
angling through the window onto the checked linoleum,
the coffee perking lazily on the gas stove, though he
muttered it would be easier to describe the color red
to someone born blind than to make clear to me
his cosmological models that, as far as I could tell,
were like gyroscopes wherein all of time twirled
just as I had once twirled in a Viennese nightclub.
That was *before* we were married, *before* the war,
before we fled from Austria to the United States
and the Institute for Advanced Study in Princeton,
traveling at night to avoid detection by the Nazis,
heading eastward via the Trans-Siberian Railway
to Japan, then across the Pacific to San Francisco
toward the most undecidable of all propositions.
But how can I even use the words *before* or *after*
when, according to Kurt, past, present and future
are simultaneous and, therefore, non-existent?

Just after we were introduced, I overheard someone
say that Gödel possessed the greatest mathematical
mind of the age. Later on, one of his acquaintances
patiently explained to me the liar's paradox—
a Cretan said "All Cretans are liars"—that lay
at the heart of his work, saying that it had to do
with certainty or its lack. I didn't care. What does
a divorced Catholic dancer whose face is marked
by a port-wine stain know of certainty anyway?
Perhaps it was that stain, rather like the sign of Cain,
that drew us together, two exiles whose only security
was within each other's arms, if there. The first time
we waltzed, he placed a finger on my left cheek,
as if to see whether the mark rubbed off like chalk,
while his other hand, moth-like, fluttered against
the small of my back. We talked about the tulips
in bloom at the Hofburg. Later we went to see them,
but they were past their peak, their petals drooping.

Even then he had strange quirks: avoiding certain foods,
anxious about his health, and afraid of people; peering
through his round spectacles at a world less real to him,
and far more frightening, than the realm of pure numbers.
Like the small invisible companion of a brilliant binary star,
I helped to hold him steady. When he insisted that his food
was poisoned, I tasted it first. When he was attacked in Vienna
by a gang of young thugs who thought he was a Jew,
I beat them back with my umbrella. When he suspected cyanide
was seeping from our refrigerator, after our move to America,
I stuck my head inside and breathed deeply as if enjoying
the sweet scent of roses. If he became agitated beyond my aid,
I'd ask Albert to take him for a walk around town

during which they would discuss their thoughts on relativity,
cosmological constants, rotating universes, and his favorite
movie, Walt Disney's *Snow White and the Seven Dwarfs*.

We were vacationing at Asbury Park on the Jersey shore
when Kurt tried to explain to me his ontological proof
for the existence of God. There was a dangerous riptide
caused by a hurricane far out to sea, so we did not swim,
instead we sat on the beach after he had beaten me
in several games of skittle ball in the boardwalk arcade,
and he began to talk of God as a positive property
or sum of perfections. When I did not understand,
he picked up a piece of driftwood and drew a formula
in the damp sand. A wave washed away the essence of x
to the third power, so he began again further up the beach
only to have a second wave deposit a little cockle shell
on the equal sign. He became upset when I started to laugh.
If God were perfect with no negatives in his essence,
I asked, how could he be aware of the two of us, human
cornucopias of fears, uncertainties and imperfections?
And what difference would divine proof make to the boy
flying a blue kite or the starfish dying above the tide line?

Knowing Kurt tended to dwell on proving God's existence
when his own seemed precarious, I reminded him gently
that he had not eaten breakfast that morning at the hotel,
suspicious of strychnine mixed into the scrambled eggs.
I took a loaf of pumpernickel bread from the picnic basket,
broke off a big piece, spread it with butter and nibbled
nonchalantly while he watched for signs of a fatal reaction.
"It's an exercise in logical investigation," he said softly,
accepting the broken bread when it appeared I would live.
"Spinoza's God is less than a person. Mine is more
than a person. He can play the role of a person."

Years after his death, I donated his papers to the Institute,
most written in German shorthand, almost undecipherable,
as if the rush of his ideas could not be captured by anything
as slow as ordinary script. In them was his ontological proof.
Other than the formula he scribbled in the sand that morning,
I never read it, nor wanted to. Love was the only proof needed.
Until my stroke made it impossible for me to save him,
spoonful by spoonful, from self-imposed starvation,
I let him know in the decipherable domestic language
of clean sheets, ironed shirts, and fresh Viennese pastry,
that no matter how many men he thought wanted him dead,
I wanted him alive. In this we agreed: not everything true
can be proven and not everything proven is true.

PSYCH WARD

Emily, all in white—
a lava dome concealed by snow
sits dormant in her room
as continental plates collide
and mantle rock turns molten
slight tremor, seismic jolt
then pyroclastic flow
aftershocks ripple out—out—

THE LANDING PLACE

In memory of the poet Hugh Ogden

He longed for all nature to be sentient,
imagining trees as benevolent psalmists
whose lengthy shadows late in the day

pointed "behind us, before, beyond,"
invoking kind shamans in streams
from whom healing wisdom flowed;

and he longed that his poems be word-sod
with the power to gestate all things new
even as his own leaf withered and died.

Weary of the constant weariness,
he retreated to his island in Maine
to hear the rustle of wind in the firs,

but could not retreat from the evergreen grief
of his lover's crushed head cradled in his lap
at the crossroads near the old railroad bed

that June day they had picked delphinium
and never saw the oncoming truck,
the blooms wilting blue into blood.

At the end, he took the worn-out trope
of thin ice and made it real, trying to reach
the mainland on skis the last day of the year,

inhaling the cold lake into his warm lungs,
frantically trying to regain the sky
as an Abnaki shaman held out a hand,

and a bull moose snagged him gently
with his mossy antlers, and a spruce nudged
him with its branch to the landing place,

where he began to dream deep down,
listening to the rooted solitude of trees
with the wordless gratitude of bone.

PRAYER BOOK
FOR
AN INFLUENZA PANDEMIC

AVIAN FLU, A PRAYER OF PETITION

*Renew our days as of old unless you have utterly
rejected us and are angry with us beyond measure.*
                    Lamentations 5:21-22

Wild swan: within whose cells
a virus incubates powerful enough
to bring down the molecular walls
of invincible Troy, we admit our unbelief
that you are the storm-strong father
of egg-hatched Helen. Nonsense!

To us, myths are agonal respirations;
Olympus, a rest home where Zeus
forgets to take his heart meds
while pecking at his cold food;
and the sibyls shuffle up and down
the hallways leaning on walkers.

Yet our fear of dying is so acute,
it sweeps away our enlightenment,
loosing a horde of superstitions
we had thought our scientific knowledge
had staked through the heart. With pockets
full of posey, we beseech you:

do not land on the waters
of a gene-pool rimmed by reeds
where another Leda waits,
but rise up on fevered wings and be gone
before your virus crosses species
and ashes, ashes, we all fall down.

H1N1, A PRAYER OF ADORATION

How deserted lies the city once so full of people.
Lamentations 1:1

Glory, laud and honor
be not unto you,
hemagglutinin and neuraminidase.
That you have twisted together
one strand human,
five strands swine,
two strands avian,
into eight RNA segments
reveals to us God's power
to make all things new
but not all things benign
toward those of us who pray
this misbegotten prayer
as fever rises in our eyes
and we sing hallelujah.

SPANISH FLU, A PRAYER OF FORGIVENESS

You have made us offscouring of the nations.
Lamentations 3:45

If this is to be a prayer
asking forgiveness
for misnaming a pandemic
during the Great War,
it is flawed from its first word
by our acute insincerity
as well as our readiness
to recommit the sin
of placing blame
anywhere else but here.
Better to identify the origin
of this appalling scourge
as a backwards nation
lax about washing hands,
than to admit it might have
started in Kansas.

SWINE FLU, A PRAYER OF CONFESSION

> *Our skin is hot as an oven.*
> *Lamentations 5:10*

Poor pig—besmirched again,
and nothing to do but squeal.
We confess we do not like you,
only your flavor dead,
though you were never
the source of this sorrow,
simply the mixing pot
for a virulent brew.
The truth is we need
a porcine scapegoat
to bear the guilt.
Similar to us humans
down to your DNA,
who else can bring home
the epidemiological bacon
better than you?

FERRET FLU,
A PRAYER OF THANKSGIVING

You make us phlegm and mucus among the peoples.
Lamentations 3:45

The news stories agree. The crossed H1N1 and avian strains may
"escape the lab," "fall into the wrong hands," "spread like wildfire,"
having the potential for both transmissibility and lethality—
the bioterrorist's dream and the epidemiologist's nightmare.
But thus far, teams of experts have concluded the mutation
"poses no immediate threat," because it makes only ferrets sick,
which puts nobody's mind at ease, certainly not the ferrets',
to whose beneficent creator we offer thanks for a "mammalian model"
with the fortuitous ability to sneeze, launching virus into the air.
May its sacrifice lead to the discovery of a vaccine that will make
prayer quaint. May it not lead to "an engineered doomsday"
where no prayer is said because no one is left to speak.

A PRAYER OF COMMEMORATION

It is of the Lord's mercies that we are not consumed.
Lamentations 3:22

Safe at the moment, the crisis past—
anti-viral drugs having forced
its retreat—we sit prayed-out
at the table, euphoric with fear's release
but chagrined by our lack of faith.
Blessed with the gift of time,
we sort through sepia-tinted photos
identifying relatives generations back.
But no one who skims this old album
with the dried-out leather cover
and the black crumbling paper
can identify who you are,
a young man in uniform with blond hair
smiling at the camera, proudly holding
your infantry hat in both hands.

Someone who cared deeply about you
placed your photo between those of
Great Aunt Edna in her wedding gown
and Great Uncle Bert holding baby Lily
in her christening dress and lace cap,
then wrote neatly beneath in white-ink
"Died March 30, 1918, Fort Riley."
Nothing more, not even on the back.
Undeniably one of us—your shy grin
brings Cousin Dave to mind—

you give a face to fifty million,
sharing with them a febrile immortality,
for the virus that pruned you from the family tree
spawned progeny who are alive and well.
As we turn the brittle page,
we touch your photo like an amulet.

A BENEDICTION

And we are not saved.
Jeremiah 8:20

May it be granted
that the one who has the last word
make it a good word,
a now-and-ever-shall-be word,
world without end. Amen

THE ART OF SCIENCE,
THE SCIENCE OF ART:
LEONARDO DA VINCI

THE PAINTING OF WINGS

> *The bird is an instrument functioning*
> *according to mathematical laws,*
> *and man has the power to reproduce*
> *an instrument like this with all its movements.*
>   *Leonardo da Vinci*

I.

More like copious field notes than paintings,
Leonardo finishes few, and even those he considers
works in progress that stopped progressing,
like lava that spewed from a fiery vent,
then congealed into a cold parody of motion.
Regretfully, he recalls his half-fledged angel,
painted years before careful observation
and anatomical sketches of hawks and swifts
riding effortlessly on rivers of wind
revealed to him that flight is achieved
by force of air, not physical strength.
Weighed down by short muscular wings
that jutted from his scapula, the angel
would have been forced to deliver
the annunciation message on foot,
trudging across a landscape, lovely yet awry,
to kneel at last before the Virgin who reads
from an out-of-perspective Bible. All wrong.

II.

Now he prepares to make amends,
not with paint but with real wings
made with reed bones and linen skin,
designed to finesse the air instead of
pummeling it into submission,
more like those of a bat than a bird.
He jots in his notebook "tomorrow morning
I shall make the strap and the attempt."
Yet he hesitates, sharing with Daedalus
a concern for catastrophic system failure,
which leads him to decide against jumping
off the roof of the Corte Vecchia,
choosing instead to launch from a cliff
beside a lake, wrapped in soft chamois
to protect his bones, with an empty wineskin
tied securely around his waist
in case the whole thing come unglued
and he plummet, like Icarus, from the sky.

III.

Leonardo deems it the boy's own fault
for not paying attention to his father's warnings
about the narrow operating parameters
and material limitations of wings,
specifically the low melting point of beeswax
if he should fly too near the sun,
and the weight of water on the feathers
if he should fly too near the waves.
But Daedalus had to share some of the blame
for perceiving of wings as nothing more
than a practical means of escape,
impervious to the joyous uprush of blue.

IV.

Darkness descends, and Leonardo recalls
his childhood dream of a hawk hovering
over his cradle, while in the refectory,
the dim glow from a lamp illumines
the scaffolding before *The Last Supper*,
and in his workshop candlelight flickers
on the clay model of a great horse,
both awaiting his hands and mind
to reach perfection, heightening his fears
that he may have miscalculated
the mathematical laws of flight,
and that the morning's planned attempt
should be postponed until he is sure
the sum does not equal his own death.

V.

As he falls asleep, he thinks he hears
the ominous vibration of wing struts.
He centers his weight, struggling
not to turn edgewise to the wind,
until all at once, in equilibrium,
he glides on the streams of the sky
before beginning a spiral descent,
landing at last by an earth-bound angel
who listens raptly to a woman reading aloud
from the *Codex on the Flight of Birds*.

THE DRAWING OF DRAGONS

If you wish to make an animal imagined by you appear natural,
let us say a dragon, take for its head that of a mastiff or hound,
with the eyes of a cat, the ears of a porcupine, the nose of a greyhound,
the brow of a lion, the temples of a rooster, the neck of a turtle.
          Leonardo da Vinci, Treatise on Painting

I.

Why should he rely on his imagination
when he has the power to transform
thought into fact, be it a bicycle,
a water wheel, a steam cannon,
or, on this sun-struck day, a baby dragon?
Might as well assemble one himself
as he has done many times before,
such as the gleaming chimera
that started out as a large lizard
he caught basking on the windowsill
to which he glued real parts:
wings sliced off a dead sparrow
and attached to the scales of its back;
sharp horns affixed to its skull;
finally melding the disparate pieces
by painting the misbegotten lizard
from head to tail with quicksilver.

II.

Nor was that doomed monstrosity
his only attempt at verisimilitude
by means of dissection and synthesis—
both effective ways to gain wisdom
if one were careful to make note
of what didn't work as well as what did.
His first success had been a gorgon
painted on a wooden shield carved
by one of his father's shareholders,
using as a model an assortment of pieces
from lizards, bats, snakes, and crickets,
cobbling them together into such a horror
that when his father had glimpsed
the painted visage, he was dismayed.
"That is what a shield ought to do,"
Leonardo had said, adding nonchalantly,
"that is what one expects from a work of art,"
as if the ability to elicit intense emotion
was a common skill among painters,
no more difficult to master than perspective.

III.

While such a visceral response might be
what Leonardo expected of a work of art,
he knew full well it was rarely achieved,
especially when combat was portrayed,
a prime example being the battle
between St. George and the dragon,
a popular subject among rich patrons,
often painted by Leonardo's predecessors
including eccentric Paolo Uccello
whose damsel had the bored demeanor
of a spectator at a dull jousting match,
and whose saint, dressed in full armor
and mounted on a white horse,
looked so cold and stiff he could benefit
from a warming blast of dragon breath
if only the dispirited beast would oblige.

IV.

Not so Leonardo's drawing of a dragon
attacking a naked warrior on horseback,
in which he had sought to capture
a brutal moment in such a way
as to force the viewer into its midst:
a cataclysm of slashing talon, teeth,
sword-stroke, and striking hoof;
a battle of balanced muscular forces
all making anatomical sense
but so savage there could be no victor,
the carnage egalitarian and total,
blood of dragon, horse and human
commingling in the carmine dust
that swirls up and out from the paper
into the viewer's startled eyes.

V.

But today Leonardo is merely sketching cats,
the whole sheet covered from top to bottom
with all types, amiably stalking, napping,
and licking their fur. Near the center
he draws the baby dragon, no model needed,
having decided to forego wings and horns,
making it more feline than reptile.
Placed beside a cat with a lion-like face,
the baby twists, turns, arches its back,
and hisses audibly in defense of its spot,
not yet knowing how to bank its fire
to keep from singeing neighborly fur,
or how to walk amicably with talons
without disturbing things with claws.

VI.

When the ink has dried, Leonardo touches
the dragon lightly to see if it will bite,
bemused by his success at capturing
in only a few ink strokes its refusal to live
peaceably among domesticated beasts,
although if it is to survive it must relent,
mastering the art of respecting boundaries
while keeping sacrosanct its own boundless space.
Smiling to himself, Leonardo wipes a tiny
drop of blood from his punctured thumb.

THE PAINTING OF WATER

> *I can give perfect satisfaction . . . in guiding*
> *water from one place to another.*
>   *Leonardo da Vinci*

I.

Even in his dreams there are rivers,
murmuring to the Maestro of Water
to study the vortices of rapids,
the swirling formation of eddies,
to sketch the velocity of floods
roaring down the Tuscan hills,
comparing their hydraulic power
to the dark force of blood coursing
through narrow arterial tunnels,
to draw as well the slow process
of streambed sedimentation similar
to the silting up of veins in old age,
revealed to him by covert dissection
and rigorous analyses as clandestine
as his ideas of evolutionary change.

II.

He wakes with a start, inundated
by too many ideas gushing
from the headwaters of his brain,
and before sunlight glints on the Adriatic
and tinctures the Apennines' eastern slopes,
he jumps from his bed and lets loose
a rivulet of sepia ink across
the flood plain of an empty page:
here winding into a design for wings,
there looping into a rotating bridge,
before diverting to vacant space
near the paper's edge where it turns
into a cataract of mirror-imaged words
about shell fossils embedded in cliffs
and geological time far more vast
than Biblical reckoning—Noah's flood
and crowded ark being replaced
by repeated submergences separated
by the slow uplift of stratified rock.

III.

Given the super-saturation of his mind,
how can he paint her young anatomy
other than as liquid panorama?
Posing for him now, La Gioconda flows,
the ripples in her sleeves like standing waves
reflecting gold, the curlicues of her hair
under a diaphanous veil identical
to swirls of spray at a waterfall's base.
Had there been no expectation by patrons
that a portrait be painted skin-side-out,
he would be delighted to draw her ribs
arching beneath the pleats of her dress,
the spreading delta of arteries and veins
within her hands, the pulse in her wrist
palpable beneath the hairs of his brush,
whispering of a hidden riparian system
more complex than that of the Arno,
which he has recently surveyed,
drawing a detailed bird's-eye-view
as part of a scheme to divert the river,
making his beloved city of Florence,
fifty miles inland, into a prosperous port,
all of which he intends to include
in the background, underpainted blue,
along with jagged peaks, green valleys,
a stone viaduct crossing a stream,
a sinuous road and a bay leading
in the distance to a New World
beckoning in a warm golden haze,

light and shade blending like sea foam,
so that while he seems to portray
a beautiful woman, as he touches
her outlined lips with the brush's tip,
he siphons into her ineffable smile
the confluence of her bloodstream
and the Earth's primordial waters,
upwelling with his own heart's awe
into a landscape beyond the curve of time.

IV.

Nearly finished,
he leaves a digit
in her left hand
incomplete,
as if he fears
a final stroke
will stop up
all of nature,
defying
the laws of motion
and stilling
the Prime Mover
who of necessity
must move
or all the world
be dead.
Dynamics
demand that
he unsettle
equilibrium;
one undone
finger,
and her heart
pumps.

THE PAINTING OF INFINITY

> *Who would believe that so small a space*
> *could contain the image of all the universe?*
> *O mighty process! . . . This is it that guides*
> *the human discourse to the considering*
> *of divine things.*
>   Leonardo da Vinci, on the camera obscura

I.

On a plastered surface underpainted
with lead-white, illumined only
by small windows high on the adjacent wall,
Leonardo compresses space,
bending his own rules of perspective
to foreshorten the ceiling and tapestries,
giving the illusory room more depth,
so that it recesses backwards to blue hills
while simultaneously rippling forwards
as if it were a continuum of the real room
in which at this moment the monks,
in their austere black and white robes,
sit at tables eating their noonday meal,
the only sound the clink of their spoons
against the bottom of their soup bowls.

II.

If only one monk, sopping up the last
of the broth with a small piece of bread,
were to glance up to where Leonardo
stands on the scaffolding with his paints,
would he be so seized by the lapis lazuli
in Christ's mantle vibrating against vermillion,
the silver-gray of Simon's sleeve edged by violet,
the azurite trembling in blue-green waves
on Philip's robe as of the sea under changing light,
that an astonished cry would rise involuntarily
from his hungry throat, startling them all
into following the direction of his gaze
to where the mute disciples are also aghast
at what they have heard but cannot believe?

III.

He asks too much of them, and of himself,
but cannot stop asking, although it is likely
that if a monk were to find words to speak,
it would be to complain about the smell of paint
or to demand that he work faster, get it done,
and be gone, as if he were a tradesman
hired to fix a cracked tile, or more like
the artist Giovanni Donato da Montorfano
who has painted the crucifixion scene
at the far end of the narrow refectory,
finishing in just one year a fresco
so jumbled that in the background
crusaders riding white warhorses mingle
with saints and sinners before a castle,
and in the foreground three crosses
soar up into the lunettes as if to pierce
the convent roof to tower over all Milan.

IV.

Better to ignore the monks now shuffling
from the room, as well as Giovanni's work,
to focus instead on painting the chasm
between the reaching hands of Judas and Christ;
not the moment of betrayal but of uncertainty
when the forces of time draw back
opening a potent vacancy wherein oscillates
the chance that Judas, in clenched desperation,
might yet resist the pull of bread and silver coin,
if only Jesus will turn his head and smile
as if to let him know he too is a beloved son;
while Jesus looks away and waits,
giving Judas the freedom to decide—
if such a freedom exists—aware that if he turns,
as he longs with all his being to do,
the light will suddenly fall at a different slant
over a Passover meal shared with good friends
on a night that will drift peacefully by,
ending in the dawn of a normal day
when no blood spills, no body breaks.

V.

And on that normal day, Leonardo finishes,
humming a jubilate to his fellow creator
who sculpts the marvel of the human eye,
that, like a camera obscura, must upend the world
in order to see. When his assistants remove
the scaffolding, he stands at a middle distance
observing the fresco whole for the first time,
its uproar of emotions conveyed by silent gesture
in incandescent hues he is certain will give off light
even if they fade and flake to pale fire,
all of it converging on one pinpoint beside
Christ's eye through which infinity glides.

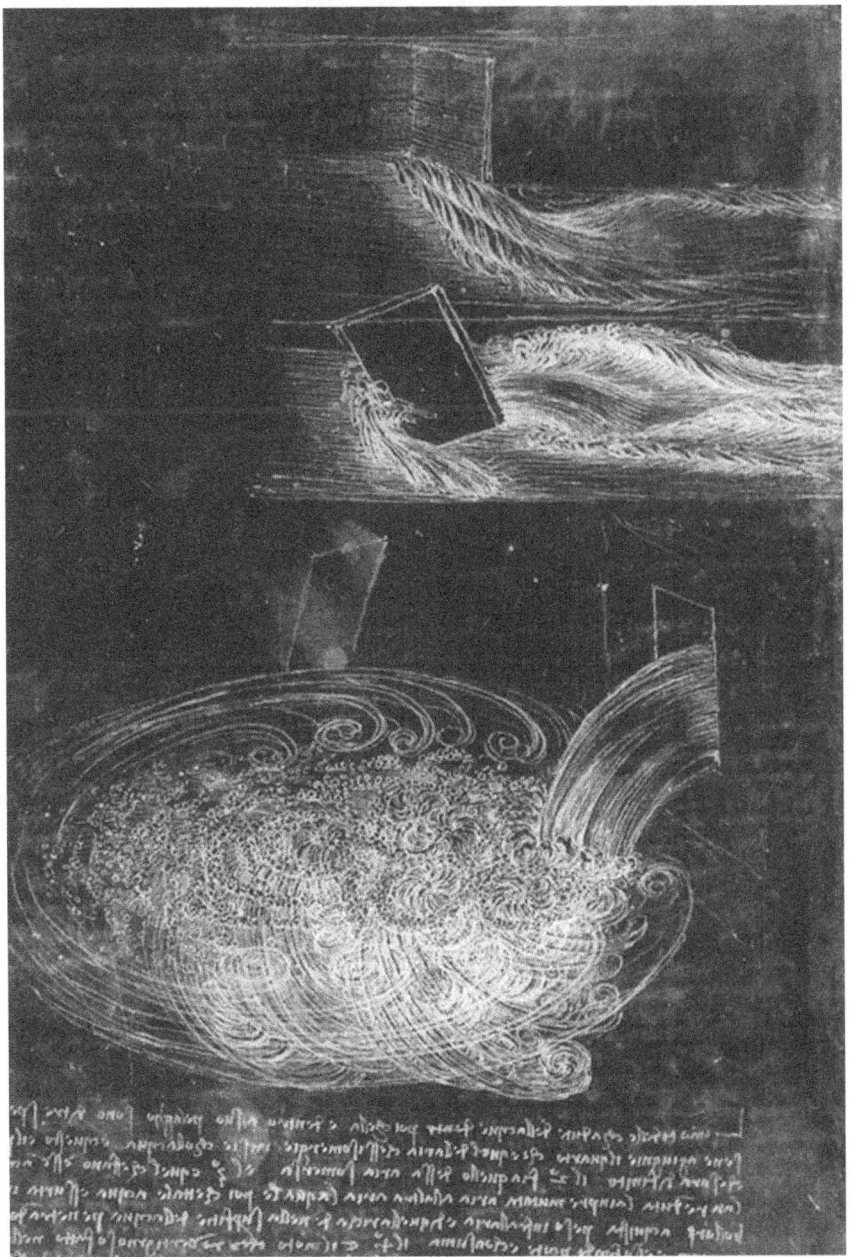

NOTES

And we are not saved. "The harvest is past, the summer has ended, and we are not saved." Jeremiah 8:20.

Psalm for a New Human Species. *Homo floresiensis* was discovered in 2003 on the island of Flores. References are to Psalm 8.

Pavane for a Dead Rover. NASA's Spirit Rover was last heard from on March 22, 2010. Its mission to Mars was supposed to last only 90 days. Instead it lasted six and a half years. Quote is from *Ulysses* by Alfred, Lord Tennyson. It is inscribed on the memorial to Robert Falcon Scott and his men on Observation Hill in Antarctica. The title echoes *Pavane for a Dead Princess* by Maurice Ravel.

Cold Comfort. Dietrich Bonhoeffer was hanged on April 9, 1945, in Flossenburg concentration camp for his involvement in the *officers' plot* against Hitler. The quote is from a letter to his friend Eberhard Bethge written from Tegel prison on February 1, 1944.

Millipede. *Pneumodesmus newmani* was discovered in 2004 by Mike Newman.

St. Ex. Antoine de Saint Exupéry was shot down by a Luftwaffe pilot on July 31, 1944. His bracelet was found in 1998. The quotes are from his books *Wind, Sand and Stars* and *The Little Prince*.

Driving the Ambulance with Robert Frost. Quotes are from Robert Frost's poem *Stopping by Woods on a Snowy Evening*.

The Mathematician's Wife Ponders Ontology. *On Undecidable Propositions of Principia Mathematica and Related Systems* by Kurt Gödel was published in 1931. It is one of the most important papers in mathematics in history. He married Adele Porkert in 1938. Gödel began work on his ontological proof in the 1940s. He considered publishing it in 1970 but hesitated out of fear of being misunderstood. First quote is from his notes to the ontological proof. By will, Gödel meant "being near=possibility of influence," and by enjoyment, he meant "life and affirmation and negation." Quote on Spinoza is from a conversation between Gödel and Hao Wang. The ontological proof is contained in *Kurt Gödel, Collected Works, Volume III, Unpublished essays and lectures*, edited by Solomon Feferman et al. (Oxford University Press, 1995).

The Landing Place. Poet Hugh Ogden drowned in Rangeley Lake, Maine, on December 31, 2006, near Oquossoc, a name that in Abnaki means the landing place. He was a professor at Trinity College in Hartford, Connecticut. Ogden had multiple sclerosis.

Prayer Book for an Influenza Pandemic. According to the World Health Organization, avian flu (H5N1) first infected humans in 1997 in China. In 2003, there was fear that wild birds, including swans, were carrying the virus from Asia into Europe. As a result, many birds were shot. In the legend of Leda and the swan, Zeus in the form of a swan rapes Leda, resulting in the birth of Helen and, ultimately, the Trojan War. The origin of the 1918 flu pandemic, which killed between 50 and 100 million people, is unknown. At the start, it was erroneously identified as originating in Spain. The first reported case in the United States was at Fort Riley, Kansas, in March 1918. In 2012, the crossing of H1N1 and H5N1 in ferrets led to a temporary research moratorium because of serious concerns about the risk of bioterrorism. In Judaism, *Lamentations* is read once a year to commemorate the destruction of the temple in Jerusalem and other profound tragedies. The translation of Lamentations 3:45 is from Rashi, the medieval Talmudic scholar and rabbi.

The Painting of Wings. The opening quote is from the *Codex Atlanticus*. The quote "tomorrow morning I shall make the strap and the attempt," is dated January 2, 1496. In his notebooks, Leonardo wrote that the attempt should be made over a lake with a wineskin for a life preserver. He also wrote that destruction could occur if "the machine breaks" or "turns edgewise." There is no record of whether the attempt actually took place. *The Annunciation* was probably painted around 1472 when Leonardo was still in Verrocchio's workshop. There is disagreement as to whether he painted it entirely, but there is agreement that he painted the angel.

The Drawing of Dragons. The stories of the lizard and the gorgon (including the quote) are told by Giorgio Vasari in his book *Lives of the Most Excellent*

Painters, Sculptors and Architects, published in 1550. The gorgon shield has been lost. The drawings are in the collection of The British Museum.

The Painting of Water. While Leonardo da Vinci was painting the Mona Lisa, he was working with Niccolò Machiavelli as a hydraulic engineer (in Italian maestro di acque) on plans to divert the Arno River with the goal of making Florence into a seaport. The recent discovery of the New World by Columbus and the subsequent voyages by the Florentine Amerigo Vespucci heightened the project's importance. Leonardo completed extensive aerial drawings and designed an earth-moving machine. However, the engineer hired to do the job radically changed the design, decreasing the depth of the canal from 30 to 14 feet. In 1504, the project was abandoned when a flood collapsed the walls and 80 soldiers drowned.

The Painting of Infinity. Leonardo's notes on the camera obscura are in the *Codex Atlanticus*. Fresco technique requires decisiveness because the tempera must be painted into fresh mortar. Because his approach to art was slow and thoughtful, he tried a new technique that, unfortunately, resulted in the painting's deterioration.

ACKNOWLEDGEMENTS

Cold Comfort, The Christian Century
Psalm for a New Human Species, The Painting of Wings, The Painting of Water,
    BioLogos (online)
Driving the Rig With Robert Frost, Ars Medica
The Mathematician's Wife Ponders Ontology, Isotope, Utah State University

Cover Art: Variations on Leonardo da Vinci's angel Gabriel from Annunciation (circa 1472-1475), Galleria Degli Uffizi, Florence, Italy.

Closing Image: Variations on Studies of Water by Leonardo da Vinci (circa 1508-1509). Royal Library, Windsor.

Kathleen L. Housley is an independent researcher, writer and poet who has written for numerous journals, including *Image, The Christian Century*, and *Metanexus* (online). In both *Firmament* (Higganum Hill Books 2007) and *Epiphanies*, she explores through poetry the borderlands between science and religion, the physical and the spiritual. This type of interdisciplinary exploration also occurs in *Keys to the Kingdom: Reflections on Music and the Mind* where she brings together neurology and music. She is also a volunteer emergency medical technician—an avocation that has provided her a unique perspective on the nature of health and wholeness.

Housley is the author of three biographies of unusual women: *The Letter Kills But the Spirit Gives Life, The Smiths* (Historical Society of Glastonbury 1993); *Emily Hall Tremaine: Collector on the Cusp* (University Press of New England 2001); and *Tranquil Power: The Art and Life of Perle Fine* (Mid-March Arts Press 2005). She is also the author of *Black Sand: The History of Titanium* (International Titanium Association 2007).

www.ingramcontent.com/pod-product-compliance
Lightning Source LLC
Chambersburg PA
CBHW032135090426
42743CB00007B/602